Fabled Forest

A "Color-and-Chronicle" Book

DUNGEON SPROUTS

© 2024 Walter Klimczak

Dungeon Sprouts Publishing

ISBN 979-833-247-6303

All Rights Reserved

www.dungeonsprouts.com

Write your name on this script of passage…

The path forward requires a touch of fate. To progress, locate a six-sided cube of chance, be it crafted or conjured.

You are an Inkslinger, an artisan mage who began an apprenticeship years ago as a humble colorist. You have just accepted a mission to explore the mystical depths of the *Fabled Forest*.

As you progress, not only will you breathe life into the realm, but add to its history and lore.

Shall we begin? Just open your backpack (it's on the next page) and whenever you find something interesting on your journey, add it to your collection. It's time for that first step...

Onward, adventurer!

Backpack

Color Test Page

Even the most skilled Inkslingers need a little practice now and then to hone their abilities. Below, you'll find a collection of empty gems. Use these to test your colors and watch your skills shine as you bring each crystal to life.

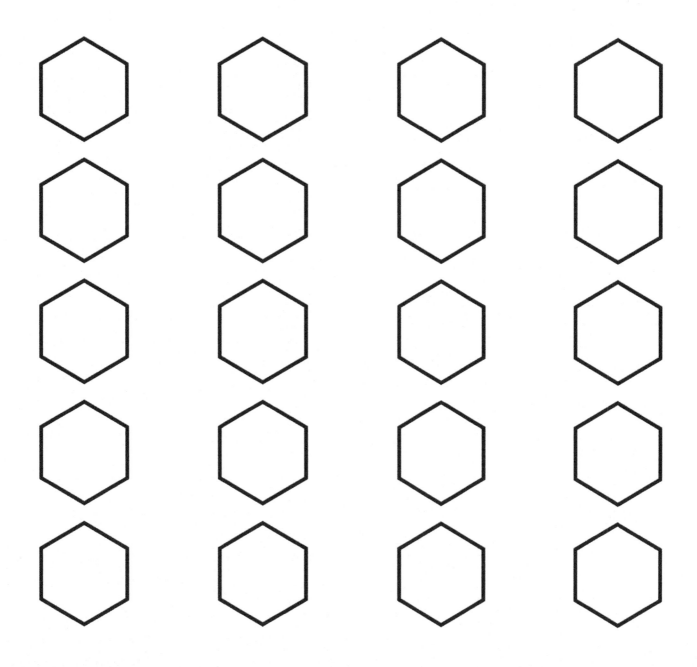

As you step into the Fabled Forest, you encounter a curious creature called a _____.

You pause for a moment at the Elder Tree. It whispers one word as you pass: _____.

A wandering peddler appears! With a sly grin, he says, "Six treasures I carry. Choose wisely, for only one can be yours."

Roll to purchase and decorate.

Excellent choice! Don't forget to place the new item safely in your backpack.

You stumble upon a fragrant ring of wildflowers! In the center, you discover _____.

A woodland sprite named _____ offers
you one wish. You ask for _____.

You've stumbled upon a pile of acorns!

If you roll ⚀ ⚂ ⚃ decorate in spring colors.

If you roll ⚁ ⚃ ⚅ decorate in fall colors.

The sound of water rushing over the smooth river stones reminds you of _____.

You discover a long-forgotten cave entrance and find
_____ hidden deep inside.

A wandering peddler appears! With a sly grin, he says, "Six treasures I carry. Choose wisely, for only one can be yours."

Roll to purchase and decorate.

Excellent choice! Don't forget to place the

new item safely in your backpack.

An owl named _____ teaches you the
forgotten magic of _____.

The forest floor is covered in many exotic flowers that have the curious aroma of _____.

You've discovered an enchanted rose bush!

If you roll  ☐ ☐ ☐ ask someone nearby what color they should be.

If you roll ☐ ☐ ☐ then you choose the color.

By combining secret herbs and leaves, you create the powerful and healing _____ tea.

An old mandolin rests against a tree. You pluck the strings and play the song _____.

A wandering peddler appears! With a sly grin, he says, "Six treasures I carry. Choose wisely, for only one can be yours."

Roll to purchase and decorate.

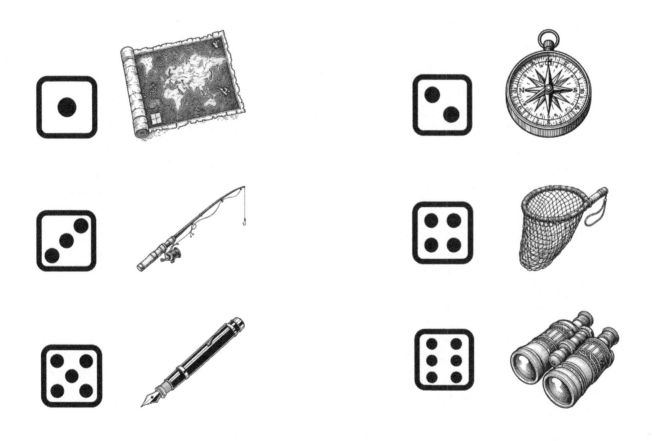

Excellent choice! Don't forget to place the

new item safely in your backpack.

An oak elf named _____ shares the
secret of creating _____.

You climb a steep hill to the Tree of Lost Memories. You finally remember _____!

Here are leaves from the Tree of Lost Memories!

If you roll  decorate in spring colors.

If you roll decorate in fall colors.

You help _____, a wounded bear. He offers you _____ for your kindness.

At twilight, a bright flash of energy fills the air. An amazing _____ appears.

A wandering peddler appears! With a sly grin, he says, "Six treasures I carry. Choose wisely, for only one can be yours."

Roll to purchase and decorate.

(if you already have an item, you can roll again)

Excellent choice! Don't forget to place the

new item safely in your backpack.

The Mirror of _____ reacts to your
touch, showing a vision of _____ .

The Great Crystal of _____ starts to
move and hum, pointing you toward a hidden path.

Crystals are growing on the ground below!

If you roll 🎲 🎲 🎲 decorate with evening colors.

If you roll 🎲 🎲 🎲 decorate with morning colors.

You place a series of colored stones on the path, then stop when you hear a voice say _____.

The words were spoken by the forest guardian, Master _____, who was greeting a wizard.

A wandering peddler appears! With a sly grin, he says, "Six treasures I carry. Choose wisely, for only one can be yours."

Roll to purchase and decorate.

(if you already have an item, you can roll again)

Excellent choice! Don't forget to place the

new item safely in your backpack.

You find an old key made of _____
and place it in your backpack in case you need it later.

You rest briefly on an old tree stump, remembering the last time you _____.

You discover magic potions behind the stump!

If you roll 🎲 🎲 🎲 decorate with colors you are wearing right now.

If you roll 🎲 🎲 🎲 decorate with colors of things you see around you.

The weather in the Fabled Forest suddenly changes. You sense that it is time to _____.

You greet a fellow Inkslinger, a kind and powerful Tale Dragon by the name of _____.

A wandering peddler appears! With a sly grin, he says, "Six treasures I carry. Choose wisely, for only one can be yours."

Roll to purchase and decorate.

(if you already have an item, you can roll again)

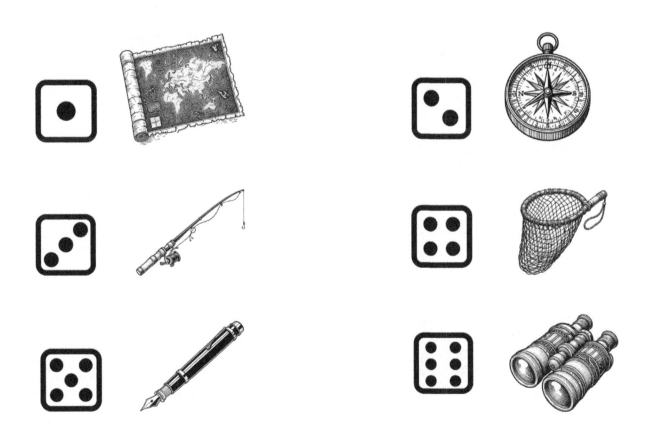

Excellent choice! Don't forget to place the new item safely in your backpack.

You leave the Fabled Forest and stop at your favorite Inn for some delicious _____. Your adventure is at an end, but the Fabled Forest will always await your return. Remember: every day is an adventure!

Fare-thee-well, Traveler!

 #dungeonsprouts
www.dungeonsprouts.com

Thank you for joining us on this journey!

Please consider leaving a review
for *Fabled Forest* on Amazon:

Your amazing support will help us craft
the best possible experiences in future
Dungeon Sprouts adventures!

Notes & Thoughts

Made in the USA
Las Vegas, NV
09 November 2024

11456699R00046